MATH SMARTS!

Problem Solving
and
Word Problem

SMARTS!

Rebecca
Wingard-Nelson

Enslow Publishers, Inc.
40 Industrial Road
Box 398
Berkeley Heights, NJ 07922
USA

http://www.enslow.com

Original edition published as *Problem Solving and Word Problems* in 2004.

Library of Congress Cataloging-in-Publication Data

Wingard-Nelson, Rebecca.
  Problem solving and word problem smarts! / Rebecca Wingard-Nelson.
     p. cm. — (Math smarts!)
  Includes index.
  ISBN 978-0-7660-3943-8
  1. Problem solving—Juvenile literature.
  2. Word problems (Mathematics)—Juvenile literature.
  I. Title.
  QA63.W5577 2012
  513—dc22

                                                                    2011006738

Paperback ISBN: 978-1-59845-325-6

Printed in China

052011 Leo Paper Group, Heshan City, Guangdong, China.

10 9 8 7 6 5 4 3 2 1

To Our Readers: We have done our best to make sure all Internet Addresses
in this book were active and appropriate when we went to press. However, the
author and the publisher have no control over and assume no liability for the
material available on those Internet sites or on other Web sites they may link to.
Any comments or suggestions can be sent by e-mail to comments@enslow.com
or to the address on the back cover.

Cover Illustration: Shutterstock.com

Contents

Introduction

If you were to look up the meaning of the word *mathematics*, you would find that it is the study of numbers, quantities, and shapes and how they relate to each other.

Mathematics is important to all world cultures, including our world of work. The following are just some of the ways in which studying math will help you:

▶ You will know how much money you are spending.

▶ You will know if the cashier has given you the right amount of change.

▶ You will know how to use measurements to build things.

▶ Your science classes will be easier and more interesting.

▶ You will understand music on a whole new level.

▶ You will be able to qualify for and land a rewarding job.

Problem solving is an important part of life. You will usually need to solve some problem every day, whether it is one that you can solve in your head or one you need a calculator to solve.

People use problem solving to find out what time they need to leave home so that they are not late. Problem solving helps you get the best value for your money by finding the better priced items and the best combinations of items.

This book has been written so that you can learn about problem solving at your own speed. You can use this book on your own or work together with a friend, tutor, or parent.

Good luck and have fun!

Addition, subtraction, multiplication, and division can be done in three different ways. You can use mental math, a paper and pencil, or a calculator to solve these types of problems.

Mental Math

You should use mental math when the numbers in the problem are easy to compute in your head, or when the problem asks for an estimate.

If you go to school 5 days a week for 40 weeks, how many days will you have gone to school?

Step 1: Write the equation.

$5 \times 40 = \underline{\quad}$

Step 2: Multiply mentally.

Think: $5 \times 4 = 20$, so $5 \times 40 = 200$

Step 3: Write the answer.

You will have gone to school 200 days.

Paper and Pencil

Some numbers are not easy to compute mentally, but they are easy to compute using a paper and pencil. In most math classes, this is the method you will use most often. Even in cases when you are going to use a calculator, you should also know how to solve the problems on paper.

When you add, subtract, multiply, or divide numbers, the operation is called a computation.

Your school year has 217 days of attendance for students. If you go to school every day for 13 years, how many days will you have attended?

Step 1: Write the problem.

$$\begin{array}{r} 217 \\ \times\ 13 \end{array}$$

Step 2: Multiply.

$$\begin{array}{r} 217 \\ \times\ 13 \\ \hline 651 \\ 2170 \\ \hline 2821 \end{array}$$

Step 3: Write the answer.

You will have attended school 2,821 days.

Calculator

There are times when a calculator is the best method of computing a problem. The numbers might be large and complicated, or you might need to have an accurate number fast. When you are using a calculator, it is important to realize you still have to know what you are trying to find and how to find it. The calculator can only compute correctly when you enter the right information.

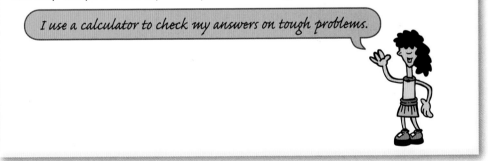

I use a calculator to check my answers on tough problems.

Unless the problem tells you what computation method to use, it is up to you to decide which computation method will be best for each problem.

There are four steps in the problem-solving process.

Step 1: Understand the Problem

Do not try to solve a problem before you understand what the problem is asking. Read the problem carefully and decide what you know and what you are trying to find.

Step 2: Make a Plan

When you understand the problem, the next step is to make a plan for solving it. Problems are solved in different ways. Will it help you to draw a picture or diagram? Is there so much data that you need to make a table or a list?

Step 3: Solve the Problem

The third step in solving a problem is to carry out your plan. Solve the problem using your plan. If it does not seem to work, choose a new plan and try again. Make sure that once you have found the answer, you write it down.

Step 4: Look Back and Check

The final step is to look back at the question and check your answer.

Pages 10–17 go into detail about each of the four problem-solving steps.

A wildlife rescue veterinarian treats wild animals that are sick or injured. The vet has kept track of the reasons for animal illness or injury in the following chart. How many more animals were treated for vehicle injuries than were treated for poisoning?

Reason for treatment	Number of cases
Gunshot	7
Poison	9
Garbage/trash injury	4
Oil spill	27
Hit by vehicle	56
Caught in trap	2

Step 1: Understand the problem.

You need to know the number of animals treated for poisoning, the number of animals treated for a vehicle injury, and the difference between them.

Step 2: Make a plan.

You can get the information to solve the problem from the table. Then you can write an equation to solve it.

Step 3: Solve the problem.

vehicle injuries − poisonings = difference

$$56 − 9 = 47$$

47 more animals were treated for vehicle injury than were treated for poisoning.

Step 4: Look back.

Reread the problem and make sure that the correct question is answered.

Do not forget to check your math!

$$47 + 9 = 56 ✔$$

The first step in solving a problem is to make sure that you understand the problem. There are questions you can use to help you read and understand a problem.

What Do You Know?

When you read the problem for the first time, you should find the key facts and details.

To help understand the problem, tell what you know about the problem in your own words.

> The school cheerleaders sold raffle tickets. There were six days of sales before the winning ticket was drawn. On the first day, Kelly sold 4 raffle tickets. Each day after that for the next 5 days, she sold 2 tickets more than she had sold the day before. How many tickets did Kelly sell in all?
>
> **Understand the problem.**
>
> **What do you know?**
>
> Key facts:
>
> 1. Kelly sold 4 raffle tickets on day 1.
>
> 2. For the next 5 days, she sold 2 more each day.

Remember: To find the right answer, you have to know the right question!

What Are You Trying To Find?

Read the problem again. What question is being asked? State the question again, this time in your own words. Decide if you have all of the information you need to solve the problem. If there is information missing, you may need to find it.

How many tickets did Kelly sell in all?

Restate the question.

What is the total number of tickets that Kelly sold?

What do you need to know to solve the problem?

In this problem you need to figure out the number of tickets Kelly sold each day.

You know that Kelly sold tickets for 6 days, 4 the first day, and 2 more each day for 5 days after that.

Now you know and understand the problem. You know there is enough information in the problem to find the answer.

Turn the page to go to the next step in solving this problem.

Sometimes it helps to leave a problem you do not understand and come back to it later.

It is important to have a plan to solve a problem. The second step in problem solving is to make a plan. For some problems a plan may be given to you, like when the problem tells you to make a table or draw a graph.

Many problems can be solved in more than one way. For others, there is only one way. It is up to you to find the best way to solve the problem.

Let's look at the same problem and make a plan to solve it.

The school cheerleaders sold raffle tickets. There were six days of sales before the winning ticket was drawn. On the first day, Kelly sold 4 raffle tickets. Each day after that for the next 5 days, she sold 2 tickets more than she had sold the day before. How many tickets did Kelly sell in all?

You can do a few different things:

1. Draw a picture.
2. Make an organized list.
3. Make a table or chart.
4. Make a graph.
5. Act out the problem.

The problem has numbers that are changing each day, so making a table or chart is a good plan.

Problem-solving strategies, or plans, are on pages 22–45. Try solving the same problem using more than one strategy, then decide which one worked best for you.

Show the information that you are given in the problem.

Day 1	**4 tickets**
Day 2	day 1 tickets + 2
Day 3	day 2 tickets + 2
Day 4	day 3 tickets + 2
Day 5	day 4 tickets + 2
Day 6	day 5 tickets + 2

You need to find the number of tickets that Kelly sold each day. Then when you have filled in the numbers in the chart, you will have what you need to add all the ticket sales together. This sounds like a good plan.

Estimate

When you are planning how to solve a problem, you can also make an estimate of what you think the answer might be. By making an estimate, you can tell what kind of answer you expect, and you can tell if your plan makes sense.

How many tickets did Kelly sell in all?

Estimate.

This is a difficult problem to estimate a close answer. You can still make some logical statements that help you know about where the answer should be.

Kelly sold at least 4 tickets each day. She sold tickets for 6 days. She sold at least $4 \times 6 = 24$ tickets.

It is easier to see a mistake when you know what kind of answer you are trying to find.

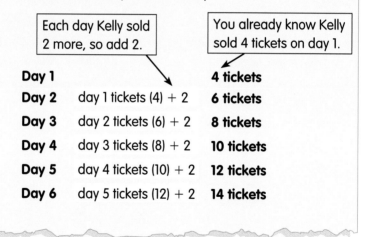

5 Solve the Problem

The third step in problem solving is to do the work, or carry out your plan. You know what the problem says and what question is being asked, and you have made a plan for answering the question.

Decide if you should use mental math, a paper and pencil, or a calculator to solve the problem.

The school cheerleaders sold raffle tickets. There were six days of sales before the winning ticket was drawn. On the first day, Kelly sold 4 raffle tickets. Each day after that for the next 5 days, she sold 2 tickets more than she had sold the day before. How many tickets did Kelly sell in all?

Solve the problem.

Step 1: Fill in the chart you made on page 13 with the number of tickets that Kelly sold each day.

Each day Kelly sold 2 more, so add 2.

You already know Kelly sold 4 tickets on day 1.

Day 1		4 tickets
Day 2	day 1 tickets (4) + 2	6 tickets
Day 3	day 2 tickets (6) + 2	8 tickets
Day 4	day 3 tickets (8) + 2	10 tickets
Day 5	day 4 tickets (10) + 2	12 tickets
Day 6	day 5 tickets (12) + 2	14 tickets

Pages 6 and 7 can help you decide which computation method—mental math, paper and pencil, or calculator—is best for solving the problem.

Step 2: The problem asks for the total number of tickets Kelly sold. From your chart you can find the number of tickets that Kelly sold each day. Add them to find the total.

$$4 + 6 + 8 + 10 + 12 + 14 = 54$$

Step 3: Write the solution. Always make sure that you change the answer of your math problem back into words so that the answer solves the original problem.

Kelly sold 54 tickets in all.

Try Again

Are you stuck? Don't give up easily; try again. Go back to the first step and try reading the problem again. You may spot important facts or details that you missed the first time. Try showing the main idea of the problem in a diagram or picture. See if you can find a pattern or break the problem into smaller steps.

Try solving the raffle ticket problem using a different plan. Decide if another plan is easier or more difficult for you.

If I cannot solve the problem after a few tries, I go to the next problem and come back later!

Make sure that you go back and answer the question in words after you solve the problem. Remember to include any units, like inches, degrees, or dollars.

You finished the problem! Hooray! But wait, there is one more important step before you stop. Always, always, always check your answer and check your work.

Check Your Answer

Make sure you answered the right question. Look at the original problem, read just the question again, and read your answer. Does your answer match the question? Estimate and use reasoning to decide if your answer makes sense.

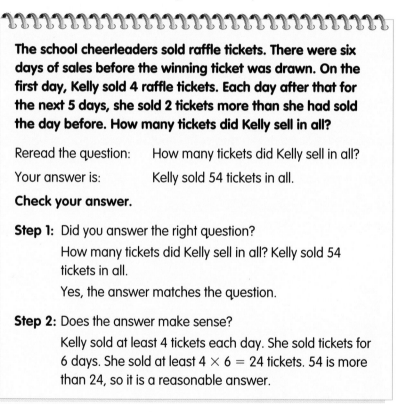

The school cheerleaders sold raffle tickets. There were six days of sales before the winning ticket was drawn. On the first day, Kelly sold 4 raffle tickets. Each day after that for the next 5 days, she sold 2 tickets more than she had sold the day before. How many tickets did Kelly sell in all?

Reread the question: How many tickets did Kelly sell in all?

Your answer is: Kelly sold 54 tickets in all.

Check your answer.

Step 1: Did you answer the right question?

How many tickets did Kelly sell in all? Kelly sold 54 tickets in all.

Yes, the answer matches the question.

Step 2: Does the answer make sense?

Kelly sold at least 4 tickets each day. She sold tickets for 6 days. She sold at least 4 × 6 = 24 tickets. 54 is more than 24, so it is a reasonable answer.

Checking your answers helps you be sure of yourself and your answers. Can you think of other ways you can check your answers?

Check Your Work

Look back at your work and compare it to the original problem. Does your work match the information in the problem?

Check and make sure that you used the correct operation. Does your operation match the operation in the original problem?

Check your math. Mistakes in easy computations happen to everyone. A double check can help get rid of computation errors.

Kelly sold 4 raffle tickets the first day. Each day after that for the next 5 days, she sold 2 tickets more than she had sold the day before. How many tickets did Kelly sell in all?

Your answer is: Kelly sold 54 tickets in all.

Check your work.

Step 1: Does your work match the original problem?

You found each day's ticket sales by adding 2 to the previous day's sales, and then added the sales together for a total.

Yes, the work matches the problem.

Step 2: Did you use the correct operation?

The words in the problem are *more than* and *total,* which show addition.

Step 3: Is your math correct?

Check your math by adding again.

The math is correct.

It is done! The problem is solved!

In real life, problems are not always as obvious as they are in math books. It is common to have information given to you that you do not need. Other times you are not given enough information to solve a problem.

Too Much Information

The first problem-solving step involves understanding the problem. In this step, you should be able to tell what information you do not need.

Duane has 4 boxes of screws that he uses for building wooden horses. There are 200 screws in each box. Each box weighs 10 kg. The horses weigh 200 kg when they are finished. Each horse uses 12 screws. How many horses can Duane build with the screws he has?

Understand the problem.

What do you know?	4 boxes of screws 200 screws per box Box of screws weighs 10 kg Horse weighs 200 kg Horse uses 12 screws
What are you trying to find?	How many horses can Duane build with the number of screws that he has?
What information is needed to solve the problem?	Number of boxes of screws Number of screws per box Number of screws per horse

Too much information can make a question confusing. It may help to write out a list of the facts in the problem, and then cross off any information that is not needed.

| What information is not needed to solve the problem? | Weight of screws
Weight of horse |

Too Little Information

Certain information must be given to you in the problem. How many hours a person has worked or the distance someone has driven are not values you can find on your own. Without all of the information needed, a problem cannot be solved.

Other times you may be expected to know information or to find it on your own. For example, the number of hours in a day is information you may be expected to know.

Bullet the bulldog weighs 23 pounds. A travel crate for pets says that it is for animals weighing no more than 350 ounces. Is Bullet too heavy for the travel crate?

Understand the problem.

What do you know?	Bullet weighs 23 pounds. The crate will hold 350 ounces.
What are you trying to find?	Is Bullet too heavy for the travel crate?
Do you have enough information?	No, you need to know how many ounces are in a pound.

Sometimes information that you are expected to know is not listed in the problem. This might include things like how many cups are in a gallon or how many inches are in a foot.

An estimate is an educated guess. It is not an exact answer. Sometimes an estimate is all you need to solve a problem.

Estimating an Answer

Decide if you need an estimate or an exact answer by reading the question carefully.

Estimates	Exact Answers
Yes or no problems	All problems that ask for an exact number
Problems that ask "Is there enough"	Problems for which the answer is crucial
Problems that ask "Is there too much"	

Danielle has $20.00. She is buying a book on CD. Does she have enough money to buy a paperback also?

Step 1: Understand the problem.

What do you know?

Danielle has $20.00.
Danielle is buying a book on CD.

Books on CD cost $12.95.
Paperbacks cost $1.95.

Bookstore Sale Poster

Paperbacks	**$1.95**
Hardcovers	**$5.95**
T-shirts	**$6.95**
Books on CD	**$12.95**

All prices include tax.

Remember: If the problem asks "Is there enough?", make your estimate high.

What are you trying to find?	Does Danielle have enough money to buy both the CD and the paperback?
Do you need an exact answer, or is an estimate close enough?	An estimate is close enough. The answer will be either yes, she has enough money, or no, she does not.

Step 2: Make a plan.

You can estimate the cost of the CD and book by rounding them to the next higher dollar and adding the whole numbers.

Step 3: Solve the problem.

$12.95 rounds to $13 $13 + $2 = $15
$1.95 rounds to $2 $15 is less than $20

Danielle has enough money to buy both the book on CD and a paperback.

Step 4: Look back.

The correct question is answered and the computations are correct.

Estimating to Check

Estimation is an important part of checking any answer. When you have an idea of what the answer should be, you know if your answer is reasonable or not.

Make up a problem using the bookstore sale that requires an exact answer.

Some word problems become easier to understand when you make an organized list. Problems that use the words *list, arrangements, combinations,* or *possibilities* are good examples of problems that may be solved by making an organized list.

A company is ordering shirts with its company logo imprinted on them. The shirts come in red and blue. They are available in small, medium, large, and extra large. How many different combinations of color and size can be made?

Step 1: Understand the problem.

What do you know?

There are 2 color choices and 4 size choices.

What are you trying to find?

How many ways can shirts be ordered?

Step 2: Make a plan.

One way to solve this type of problem is to make an organized list. You can list the possible shirts that can be made.

Organized lists can help you understand the problem or solve it.

There are two color choices and four size choices. Make a list of each color, in each size. To keep the list organized, first list all the sizes in one color, and then list all the sizes in the other color.

	Color	Size
1.	Red	Small
2.	Red	Medium
3.	Red	Large
4.	Red	Extra Large
5.	Blue	Small
6.	Blue	Medium
7.	Blue	Large
8.	Blue	Extra Large

Step 3: Solve the problem.

By reading the problem again, you can see that the problem asked for the number of different shirts that can be made. The list is not the answer to the problem. From the list you can find the answer by counting the number of items listed.

Answer: There are 8 different shirts that can be ordered.

Step 4: Look back.

Make sure you have listed all the possible colors and sizes in each color. Check to make sure you have answered the question and not just created a list.

HEY! That was easy!

10 Look for a Pattern

A pattern is the way something is arranged or repeated. Some problems are solved best by finding a pattern. Once you find a pattern, you can predict what will happen next.

The diagram shows a pattern of first a round bead, then two oval beads. The pattern repeats itself three times. It is reasonable to predict the next bead to go on the string will be a round bead.

Patterns can also be found in tables of numbers. When you are looking for a pattern in a table, compare the value in one row or column to the value in the next.

Day	Exercise Time in minutes
1	15
2	20
3	25
4	30

Compare the first day's time to the second day's time. The second day is 5 minutes longer.

Patterns repeat themselves. If the numbers change each time in the same way, then the table shows a pattern. This table shows that each day the exercise time is 5 minutes longer than the day before. Each row changes in the same way, so it is a pattern.

Look for patterns in equations, graphs, and tables.

24

The costs associated with being a member of a DVD club are given in the table. What will the total cost be when 5 DVDs are purchased?

Number of DVDs	Total cost ($)
1	41
2	52
3	63
4	74
5	?

Step 1: Understand the problem.

You know the cost associated with the purchase of the given number of DVDs.

You want to know what the total cost will be for 5 DVDs.

Step 2: Make a plan.

Look for a pattern in the table. Compare the cost of buying 1 DVD to the cost of buying 2 DVDs.

$52 ←—— 2 DVDs
$- \$41$ ←—— 1 DVD
$11 ← difference

Does the pattern continue?

$63 ←—— 3 DVDs
$- \$52$ ←—— 2 DVDs
$11 ← difference

Yes, for each additional DVD, the cost increases by $11.

Step 3: Solve the problem.

The cost of 5 DVDs is $11 more than the cost of 4 DVDs. 4 DVDs cost $74.

$\$74 + \$11 = \$85$

The total cost of 5 DVDs is $85.

Step 4: Look back.

The answer matches the question, and the computation matches the pattern in the table.

To find a pattern, you must have more than one example. A change becomes a pattern when the same change keeps repeating.

When you make a table, you put information into an easy-to-read format. This will help you keep track of data, spot missing data, and identify data that is needed to solve the problem.

Jose wants to save $48.00 from his job. Each week he earns a little more than the week before. He decides to save $8.00 the first week, and $1.00 more each week after. How many weeks will it take to save $48.00?

Step 1: Understand the problem.

What do you know?   Jose wants to save $48.00.
He is saving $8.00 the first week.
Each week he saves $1.00 more than he did the previous week.

What are you trying to find?   How many weeks will it take to save $48.00?

Step 2: Make a plan.

Make a table to organize the amounts Jose saves each week and his total savings. Label the rows and columns in your table. Fill in the data that you know. You know that Jose saved $8 the first week.

Week	1	2	3	4	5	6
Weekly Savings	$8					
Total Savings						

When you make a table, see if you can find a pattern in the information in the table.

Step 3: Solve the problem.

Add $1.00 more to each week's savings. Week 1 savings was $8, so week 2 is $9. Continue the pattern.

Week	1	2	3	4	5	6
Weekly Savings	$8	$9	$10	$11	$12	$13
Total Savings						

Now start adding the total savings. After week 1, Jose saved $8. Write $8 in total savings.

For week 2, add the total from week 1, $8, to the savings from week 2, $9. $8 + $9 = $17. Continue adding for each week.

Week	1	2	3	4	5	6
Weekly Savings	$8	$9	$10	$11	$12	$13
Total Savings	$8	$17	$27	$38	$50	$63

Jose will save $38 by week 4. That is not enough. By week 5 he will have saved a total of $50. This is the first week he will have reached his goal of $48.

It will take Jose 5 weeks to save $48.

Step 4: Look back.

Check your calculations in the table. Are they correct? Yes. Does your answer seem reasonable? Yes.

Look over the problems you have solved. By knowing what types of problems you have solved using certain strategies, you can recognize how to solve new problems that are similar.

Sometimes you make a graph to solve a problem. A graph can help you understand the information by showing it clearly. Problems that ask you to compare information can be solved by graphing the data.

Two landscaping companies, Rockford Lawns and Monarch Landscaping, counted their jobs from May to August. Which company showed the steadiest growth?

Number of Jobs by Month

Month	Rockford	Monarch
May	40	50
June	90	70
July	70	80
August	40	90

Step 1: Understand the problem.

What do you know? — You know the number of jobs each company did each month.

What are you trying to find? — You want to compare the growth of the companies to figure out which showed a steadier growth.

Step 2: Make a plan.

You can put the data from the table into a graph and compare the two companies.

Graphs are best when a problem gives you data about an event, or the question in the problem can be answered by "seeing" a pattern in the data.

Step 3: Solve the problem.

A line graph can chart each company's growth over time. You can put both lines on the same graph to compare the companies.

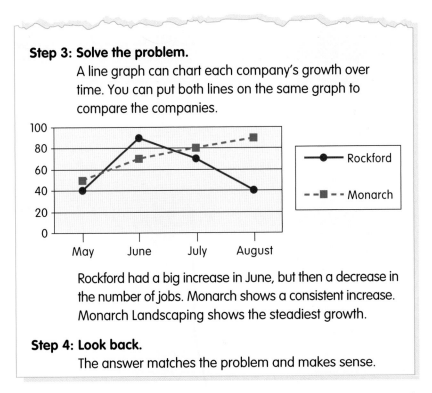

Rockford had a big increase in June, but then a decrease in the number of jobs. Monarch shows a consistent increase. Monarch Landscaping shows the steadiest growth.

Step 4: Look back.

The answer matches the problem and makes sense.

There are many types of graphs that you can use to display information. A bar graph uses bars to compare data or show a trend.

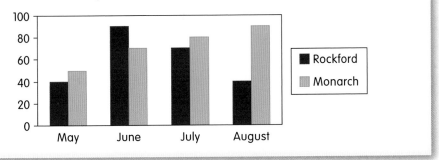

When you are graphing more than one set of data on the same graph, a legend can be used to label the data sets.

13 Draw a Diagram

Diagrams can be useful in problems that show how information can be combined. For example, you may wish to find out how many different outfits can be made from two pairs of pants and three shirts.

Five teams are to play each other one time each in a volleyball tournament. How many games are needed?

Step 1: Understand the problem.

What do you know?	There are 5 teams. Each team will play each other team one time.
What are you trying to find?	How many games will be played all together?

Step 2: Make a plan.
Draw a diagram with 5 teams, then draw a line from each team to each other team.

Step 3: Solve the problem.
Count the lines connecting the teams. There are 10 connections, so 10 games need to be played.

TEAM
1
2
3
4
5

Step 4: Look back.
The answer matches the question and appears correct.

The classic "trick" problem on the next page can show how helpful drawing a diagram can be.

Drawing pictures can clear up a problem!

A snail is climbing up a 6-foot slope. Each day, the snail moves 2 feet up the slope, but it slides back 1 foot every night. How many days will it take the snail to reach the top of the slope?

Step 1: Understand the problem.

What do you know? — The slope is 6 feet. Each day the snail goes forward 2 feet and back 1 foot.

What are you trying to find? — On what day will the snail reach the top of the slope?

Step 2: Make a plan.

At first glance, it appears that each day the snail moves 1 foot. It should take 6 days, but you want to be sure, so draw a diagram.

Step 3: Solve the problem.

Draw a picture of the slope, with an arrow forward for each day and an arrow back for each night.

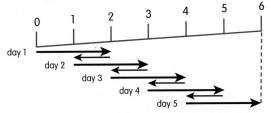

The diagram shows that the snail will reach the top of the slope on the 5th day. Without sliding back that night, the snail will gain 2 feet the final day instead of only 1 foot. It will take the snail 5 days to reach the top.

Step 4: Look back.

Check your diagram for accuracy.

Pictures and diagrams help you understand the problem and avoid careless mistakes. The picture can be as simple or as detailed as you need it to be.

Working backward is best when you know how something ends but need to know how it began. Some of the problems you can work backward to solve include:

What time should I leave home to get somewhere on time?
When should I start my report if it is due in three weeks?

Suppose you need to be home at 9:30 P.M., and it takes 1 hour and 20 minutes to drive home. What time should you leave?

Step 1: Understand the problem.
You know you need to be home at 9:30 P.M. and it will take 1 hour and 20 minutes to drive home.

Step 2: Make a plan.
You can draw a picture to help work backward and find the time you need to leave.

Step 3: Solve the problem.
9:30 P.M. minus 1 hour and 20 minutes is 8:10 P.M.

You need to leave at 8:10 P.M.

Time you need to leave   Time you need to be home 9:30 P.M.

Subtract 1 hour and 20 minutes.

Step 4: Look back.
8:10 P.M. plus 1 hour and 20 minutes is 9:30 P.M.

To work backward, it may be helpful to draw a timeline or a picture that shows the order of events. Then begin at the end and work toward the beginning.

Be careful when you are adding and subtracting time units. There are 60 minutes in one hour.

Jordan is going into 9th grade and weighs 119 pounds. He gained 9 pounds while he was in 8th grade. How much did Jordan weigh when he was beginning 8th grade?

Step 1: Understand the problem.

You know Jordan weighs 119 pounds now. You want to know what he weighed when he was going into 8th grade.

Step 2: Make a plan.

Since you know an ending weight and want to find a starting weight, working backward is a good plan. You can draw a timeline to show the changes.

Step 3: Solve the problem.

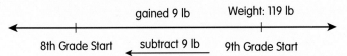

Begin with the end weight of 119 pounds and work backward in time. Jordan gained, or added weight, which indicates addition. When working backward, use the inverse operation, so subtract the weight.

$$119 - 9 = 110$$

Jordan weighed 110 pounds when he began 8th grade.

Step 4: Look back.

Check the computations. Begin with your answer and go forward in time.

$$110 + 9 = 119$$

To check a problem you worked backward, use your answer and work forward. For more on inverse operations, see the bottom of page 47.

In some problems you can use what you know to draw a conclusion about what you are not told. For example, if you know that Aunt Sally has red hair, you can use logical reasoning to say that Aunt Sally does not have brown, black, or blond hair.

Logic Tables

Logic tables or charts can help you organize information. Fill in the chart with the information you know, using *yes* for positive information and *no* for negative information.

> **There are five people in the Jacobs family. They are Emily, Jason, Maureen, Sarah, and Tim. Their ages are 3, 6, 10, 32, and 36. Maureen is the oldest and Emily is the youngest. Tim is 10, but Jason is not 6. How old is Sarah?**
>
> **Step 1: Understand the problem.**
> You want to know Sarah's age.
>
> **Step 2: Make a plan.**
> There is a lot of information, and you can use it to draw conclusions. You can make a logic table to organize the information.
>
> **Step 3: Solve the problem.**
> Draw a table to organize the information. Then fill in the table with the information that you are given in the problem.

Once you have the information organized, it becomes easier to draw conclusions.

	3	6	10	32	36
Emily	Yes	No	No	No	No
Jason	No	No	No		No
Maureen	No	No	No	No	Yes
Sarah	No		No		No
Tim	No	No	Yes	No	No

Then use reasoning. You know that each person can be only one age, and that no two people in the family are the same age.

Each row or column must have only one *yes*. Fill in the empty spaces in the columns and rows that have one *yes* with a *no*.

	3	6	10	32	36
Emily	Yes	No	No	No	No
Jason	No	No	No	Yes	No
Maureen	No	No	No	No	Yes
Sarah	No		No	No	No
Tim	No	No	Yes	No	No

Now the problem is easy You can see that there is only one age that Jason can be by looking in the row that has his name. Jason has to be 32.

There is only one blank space left, and it is Sarah's age. Sarah is 6 years old.

Step 4: Look Back.

Do all the clues you have been given match your answer? Yes, so the answer is correct.

Wow!
Anyone can do this!

Looking back to check your clues is very important. Check each clue against the conclusion that you have drawn to make sure they do not disagree.

Problems can sometimes be made simpler by changing the numbers or breaking the problem apart.

Smaller Numbers

When the numbers in the problem make it seem overwhelming, try using smaller numbers, or a series of smaller numbers, to help you find a pattern.

Sam is building a fence in 32 sections with a post on each section's end. How many posts does Sam need?

Step 1: Understand the problem.
Sam needs 32 sections of fence. The question asks how many posts she needs.

section   post

Step 2: Make a plan.
You can use smaller numbers of sections and see if there is a pattern.

Step 3: Solve the problem.
How many posts does Sam need for:

| 1 section? | 2 posts | 3 sections? | 4 posts |
| 2 sections? | 3 posts | 4 sections? | 5 posts |

The pattern shows that Sam needs one more post than she has sections of fence. She needs $32 + 1 = 33$ posts.

Step 4: Look back.
The right question is answered and the answer makes sense.

Problem-solving plans can be used together. The problem on this page used a simpler problem, a picture, and a pattern.

Break It Apart

When the problem gives you lots of information and there is more than one computation that needs to be done, you can break the problem into smaller parts.

Jacob works 4 hours every weekday, and 6 hours on Saturday. He earns $8.25 an hour. How much does Jacob earn in a week?

Step 1: Understand the problem.
How much money does Jacob earn in a full week?

Step 2: Make a plan.
Jacob works a different number of hours on different days, but he earns the same amount per hour. You can break the problem into smaller problems.

Step 3: Solve the problem.
Smaller problem 1: How many hours does Jacob work over the weekdays? There are 5 days in a week, and he works 4 hours each day, so that is $5 \times 4 = 20$ hours.

Smaller problem 2: How many hours does Jacob work in a full week? Weekday hours + weekend hours = total
$20 + 6 = 26$ hours in a full week.

Smaller problem 3: Now that you know the answers to the first two smaller problems, how much Jacob earns in a week is a small problem also.
Hours $\times$ pay rate = pay $26 \times \$8.25 = \$214.50$
Jacob earns $214.50 per week.

Step 4: Look back.
Check your math by working backward or by using a calculator.

Always be sure you are doing all four problem-solving steps!

Guess and Check or Brainstorm

Sometimes you may not be able to decide how to solve a problem. The problem may have large numbers or lots of information. The problem may even give you the solution, like a multiple choice problem. It may just seem that no matter what strategy you choose, you cannot find the solution.

Guess and Check

You may guess the answer, test it to see if it is correct, and make another guess if the answer is not correct.

George knows he needs either 5, 6, or 7 sheets of plywood to finish a wall. The wall has an area of 180 square feet, and each sheet of plywood covers 32 square feet. How many sheets does George need?

Step 1: Understand the problem.
How many sheets of plywood are needed to cover 180 square feet? Each sheet covers 32 square feet.

Step 2: Make a plan.
You know the answer is either 5, 6, or 7, so you can guess an answer and check from there.

Step 3: Solve the problem.
First guess whether 6 sheets will be enough. If each covers 32 square feet, then 6 sheets will cover $6 \times 32 = 192$ square feet. That is more than George needs, so check and see if 5 is enough.

$$5 \times 32 = 160 \text{ square feet.}$$

If your first guess is not right, you can still use what you have learned to help you make a closer guess next time. If your guess was too high, try a lower number!

5 is not enough. George needs 6 sheets of plywood to finish the wall.

Step 4: Look back.

You have answered the right question, and you have checked the answer using guess and check.

Brainstorming

Brainstorming is looking at a problem in new and different ways. Be creative, be imaginative, and start looking at the problem from a different direction.

Tim and Tony are brothers, have the same mother and father, and were born on the same day, but they are not twins. How is this possible?

Step 1: Understand the problem.

How can the boys not be twins?

This is fun!

Step 2: Make a plan.

Use brainstorming to find the answer.

Step 3: Solve the problem.

You know the boys have the same parents and the same birthday, but are not twins. They must have more siblings born on the same day, so they may be triplets or quadruplets.

Step 4: Look back.

The answer makes sense and answers the question.

Brainstorming works really well in a group. People with different ideas can help each other think in new ways.

Variables and Formulas

In mathematics, a blank space or blank line is often at the place of the number that you do not know or are trying to find.

$$2 + \underline{} = 5$$

Variables

In algebra, a variable takes the place of the number that you do not know or are trying to find.

$$2 + c = 5$$

Four times a certain number can be written as $4n$, or $4 \times n$.
The variable n represents the number you do not know or are trying to find.

Variables that are alike can be added or subtracted. To add like variables, add the numbers in front of the letters.

$$t + t = 2t$$
$$2c + c = 3c$$

To subtract like variables, subtract the numbers in front of the letters.

$$4r - r = 3r$$
$$3d - 2d = d$$

Variables that are not alike cannot be added or subtracted.

$$2r + s$$
$$5x - 2y$$

That would be like adding apples and . . . hamburgers!

A variable next to a number means multiplication.
$$3d \text{ is the same as } 3 \times d$$

Formulas

A formula is a special equation that uses variables. The values that are given to you in a problem can be substituted into the formula to find the unknown value.

For example, the formula for the perimeter of a square is $p = 4s$. The variable p stands for perimeter and s stands for side length.

Find the perimeter of a square with a side length (s) of 3 inches.

Step 1: Write the formula. $p = 4s$

Step 2: Substitute the number you $p = 4(3 \text{ inches})$
know for the side length.

Step 3: Write the solution. $p = 12 \text{ inches}$

The perimeter of the square is 12 inches.

The formula for the area of a rectangle is $A = bh$. The variable A stands for area, b stands for base, and h stands for height.

What is the base of a rectangle that has a height of 2 feet and an area of 12 square feet?

Step 1: Write the formula. $A = bh$

Step 2: Substitute in the known values. $12 \text{ square feet} = b(2 \text{ feet})$

Step 3: Divide both sides of the equation by 2 feet to get the variable by itself.

$$\frac{\overset{6}{\cancel{12}} \text{ square feet}}{\cancel{2} \text{ feet}} = \frac{b(\cancel{2} \text{ feet})}{\cancel{2} \text{ feet}}$$

Step 4: Write the solution.
$6 \text{ feet} = b$
The base of the rectangle is 6 feet.

Formulas are used to find temperatures, areas, volumes, and rates of speed; to calculate interest; and to mix chemicals.

An algebraic expression connects numbers or variables with operators. Operators are signs such as $+$, $-$, $\times$, and $\div$ that show addition, subtraction, multiplication, and division. The equal sign ($=$) is not an operator. Algebraic expressions do not contain an equal sign.

Some algebraic expressions are:

$$a + 3 \qquad x - y \qquad 120rt$$
$$9 \times u \qquad p \div 2 \qquad ab - 78c$$

For multiplication of a number and a variable, the multiplication symbol is often not shown but is understood to be there.

$$2t \text{ is the same as } 2 \times t$$
$$rs \text{ is the same as } r \times s$$

Division is often shown with a horizontal line or a slash. It may look like a fraction to you.

$$\frac{2}{x} \text{ is the same as } 2 \div x$$
$$\frac{y}{3} \text{ is the same as } y \div 3$$

Many times a phrase that is written in words can also be written as an algebraic expression.

Words	Algebraic Expression
Three plus a number	$3 + x$
Six times a number	$6n$
Half of a number	$a \div 2$

Half of a number is the same as dividing a number by 2.
A third of a number is the same as dividing a number by 3.
Twice means multiply by 2.

Evaluating an Expression

To *evaluate* an expression means "to find the value of" the expression. Just replace each variable with its value. Then the operations can be performed. When you are evaluating an expression, the order of operations is:

P—Perform all operations inside **P**arentheses
E—**E**xponents
M—**M**ultiply
D—**D**ivide
A—**A**dd
S—**S**ubtract

If $r = 5$ and $s = 3$, evaluate each of the following expressions:
$r + s$, $3r - rs$

Step 1: Write the first expression.	$r + s$
Step 2: Substitute in the known values.	$5 + 3$
Step 3: Perform any operations using the order of operations.	8
Step 4: Write the solution.	$r + s = 8$

Repeat the steps for the second expression.

Step 1: Write the expression.	$3r - rs$
Step 2: Substitute in the known values.	$3(5) - (5)(3)$
Step 3: Perform any operations in order. First multiply. Then subtract.	$15 - 15$ 0
Step 4: Write the solution.	$3r - rs = 0$

evaluate an expression — To find the value of an expression.

Often the fastest and easiest way to solve a problem is to write an equation that matches the problem.

An equation is a math sentence. It says that one expression has the same value as another expression or a number. An algebraic equation uses the equal sign (=).

Some algebraic equations are:

$$3x = 9$$
$$y + 4 = 2y$$

Some word sentences can be changed into algebraic equations.

Word Sentence	Algebraic Equation
A number divided by 4 equals 9.	$t \div 4 = 9$
16 is 3 years older than I am.	$16 = m + 3$

Writing an Algebraic Equation

Key words in a sentence tell you what operation is being performed and where the equal sign belongs. *Equals* and *is* are key words for the equal sign.

Write a word sentence first. Choose variables (letters) to stand for the numbers you do not know. Use symbols and operators for the key words in the sentence. Replace each word or phrase with a number, variable, or symbol.

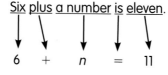

Six plus a number is eleven.

$$6 \quad + \quad n \quad = \quad 11$$

Key words for each operation are found on pages 46–53.

A number <u>minus</u> <u>1</u> <u>equals</u> <u>4</u>.

$$x \quad - \quad 1 \quad = \quad 4$$

Word problems are not always written in a sentence that can be changed easily to an algebraic equation. Rewrite the problem as a sentence that uses words you can change to algebra.

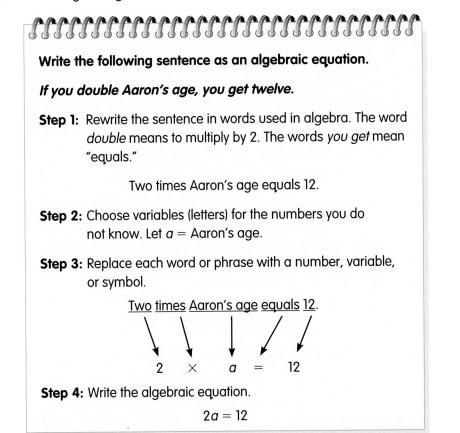

Write the following sentence as an algebraic equation.

If you double Aaron's age, you get twelve.

Step 1: Rewrite the sentence in words used in algebra. The word *double* means to multiply by 2. The words *you get* mean "equals."

Two times Aaron's age equals 12.

Step 2: Choose variables (letters) for the numbers you do not know. Let a = Aaron's age.

Step 3: Replace each word or phrase with a number, variable, or symbol.

<u>Two</u> <u>times</u> <u>Aaron's age</u> <u>equals</u> <u>12</u>.

$$2 \quad \times \quad a \quad = \quad 12$$

Step 4: Write the algebraic equation.

$$2a = 12$$

Use variables for numbers that are missing or that you are trying to find.

Word problems contain key words that tell you what type of operation to perform. Many words in a word problem indicate addition. Some key words and phrases for addition are:

add	combined	more than
additional	exceeds	plus
all	gain	raise
all together	greater	sum
and	in addition to	together
both	in all	total

Use the key words to change a problem from a word sentence into an algebraic equation. Write the sentence in words first, then change it to an equation.

<u>5</u> <u>combined with</u> <u>a certain number</u> <u>is</u> <u>29.</u>

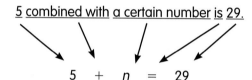

$$5 \quad + \quad n \quad = \quad 29$$

If a problem does not have a sentence that is easy to change to an equation, use the key words you know to write a sentence.

Jim is 15 years old. The sum of Jim's and Tom's ages is 32 years.

Write an algebraic equation to model the problem.

Step 1: Read the problem. What key words are used?

The word *sum* tells you that this is an addition problem. The phrase *the sum of* tells you that what comes next is added.

Problems that show "some, then some more" are addition problems. Tina's car odometer was at 4,200 miles, then she went on vacation. Now the odometer is at 5,721 miles. The odometer was at "some" miles, then added "some more."

Step 2: Write a sentence in words that shows what the problem is saying.

Jim's age plus Tom's age is 32.

Step 3: Change the word sentence to an equation. Use a variable for the number you are trying to find (Tom's age, t). Replace the words with the values that you are given (Jim's age is 15).

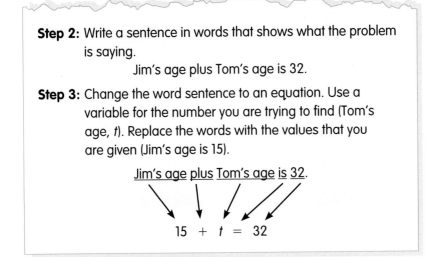

Solving Addition Problems

To solve an algebraic equation, you need to get the variable by itself on one side of the equal sign.

You can use subtraction to get the variable t by itself because subtraction is the inverse operation of addition. Subtract the same number (15) from both sides of the equation.

$$15 + t = 32$$
$$\cancel{15} + t - \cancel{15} = 32 - 15$$
$$t = 17$$

Since $t = 17$, Tom's age is 17. Remember to check your answer. Replace the variable in the original equation with your solution.

$$15 + t = 32$$
$$15 + 17 = 32$$
$$32 = 32 \checkmark$$

Inverse operations:
Addition and subtraction are inverse operations.
Multiplication and division are inverse operations.

Some key words and phrases that tell you the problem is a subtraction problem are:

changed	have left	reduced
comparison	left	remain
decreased by	less than	subtract
difference	lost	take away
dropped	minus	

Other key words that show subtraction are words that end in *er*.

fewer	higher	larger	longer

Sara's dog had puppies. Three of the puppies have been sold. There are four puppies left. How many puppies did Sara's dog have?

Write an algebraic equation to model the problem.

Step 1: Read the problem. What key words are used?

The words *have been sold* and *left* tell you that this is a subtraction problem. There were some puppies and some went away.

Step 2: Write a sentence in words that shows what the problem is saying.

Total puppies minus puppies sold equals puppies left.

Step 3: Change the word sentence to an equation. Use a variable for the number you are trying to find (total puppies, *p*). Replace the words with the values that you are given (puppies sold, 3; puppies left, 4).

<u>Total puppies</u> <u>minus</u> <u>puppies sold</u> <u>equals</u> <u>puppies left</u>

$$p - 3 = 4$$

Remember: Always check your solutions by replacing the variable with your answer in the original equation. Be sure your answer makes sense for the problem.

Solving Subtraction Problems

The inverse of subtraction is addition. Use addition to get the variable by itself in a subtraction problem.

Trace has 15 comic books, which is 6 fewer books than Ryan. How many comic books does Ryan have?

Step 1: Read the problem. What key words are used?

Fewer shows subtraction.
The phrase *which is* stands for "equals."

Step 2: Write a sentence in words that shows what the problem is saying.

Trace's comic books (15) equals Ryan's comic books (*r*) minus 6.

Step 3: Write the algebraic equation.

$$15 = r - 6$$

Step 4: Add to get the variable (*r*) by itself on one side of the equation.

$$15 = r - 6$$
$$\underline{+6 = +6}$$
$$21 = r$$

Step 5: Write the solution.
Ryan has 21 comic books.

$$r = 21$$

Step 6: Check the solution. Replace the variable with your solution.

$$15 = r - 6$$
$$15 = 21 - 6$$
$$15 = 15 \checkmark$$

Make up some addition and subtraction word problems. Explain which key words tell you they are addition or subtraction problems.

Some key words that tell you multiplication is being used are:

at	of	rate
every	per	times
multiply	product	twice

Another clue that multiplication is being used is when the problem asks you to change between one unit and multiple units. For example:

If you know:	**and you need to find:**
Price of one	Price of many
Size of one	Size of many
Length of one	Length of many

Sharon sold boxes of chocolate at a profit of $2.50 per box. Sharon's total profit was $75.00. How many boxes of chocolate did she sell?

Write an algebraic equation to model the problem.

Step 1: Read the problem. What key words are used?
The key word *per* shows multiplication. *Total profit was* tells you where the equal sign belongs.

Step 2: Write a word sentence that shows what the problem is saying.
Profit of $2.50 per box times the number of boxes sold equals total profit.

Step 3: Change the word sentence to an equation. Use a variable for the number you are trying to find (number of boxes sold, *b*). Replace the words with the values that are given in the problem.
$$\$2.50 \times b = \$75.00$$

Be careful when negative numbers are being multiplied. Do not confuse them with subtraction. $-4n = 24$ is the same as $(-4) \times (n) = 24$
To solve the equation, divide both sides by -4.

Solving Multiplication Problems

Division is the inverse of multiplication. To get a variable that is being multiplied alone on one side of the equation, you divide.

Joe is building chairs. Each chair has 4 legs. How many chairs can Joe make with 72 legs?

Step 1: Read the problem. What clues are used?

The problem goes from the number of legs for one chair (4) to the number of legs (72) for many chairs. Changing from one to many shows multiplication.

Step 2: Write a word sentence, then write an algebraic equation.

One chair's legs times the number of chairs equals the total number of legs.

$$4c = 72$$

Step 3: Use division to get the variable (c) by itself on one side of the equation.

$$4c = 72$$
$$\frac{\cancel{4}c}{\cancel{4}} = \frac{\cancel{72}^{18}}{\cancel{4}}$$

Step 4: Write the solution.
Joe can make 18 chairs.

$$c = 18$$

Step 5: Check the solution. Replace the variable with your solution.

$$4c = 72$$
$$4 \times 18 = 72$$
$$c = 18$$

Remember: To solve an equation, you need to get the variable by itself. It does not matter which side of the equation the variable is on. For both $3s = 54$ and $54 = 3s$, the value of s is 18.

Look for these key words and phrases to help you recognize division word problems:

average	equal parts	quotient
cut	evenly	separate
divided	every	shared
divisor	out of	split
each		

Another way you can tell that a problem is using division is when the problem gives you many and asks for one.

If you know:	**and you need to find:**
Price of many	Price of one
Size of many	Size of one
Length of many	Length of one

A teacher divided a large container of peanuts into 7-ounce containers for his students. No peanuts were left in the large container. If there are 18 students, how many ounces of peanuts were in the large container?

Step 1: Read the problem. What key words are used?
The key word *divided* tells you that division is used.
There are tells you where the equal sign belongs.

Step 2: Write a sentence in words that shows what the problem is saying.

Large container weight divided by small container weight equals number of containers.

The number of containers is also the number of students.

When both sides of an equation are multiplied by the same number, both sides will still be equal.

Step 3: Change the word sentence to an equation. Use a variable for the number you are trying to find (large container weight, *c*). Replace the words with the values that are given in the problem (small container weight is 7 ounces; number of containers is 18).

$$c \div 7 = 18, \text{ or } \frac{c}{7} = 18$$

Solving Division Problems

The inverse of division is multiplication. Use multiplication to get the variable *c* by itself.

Multiply both sides of the equation by 7.

$$c \div 7 = 18$$
$$c \div 7 \ (\times 7) = 18 \times 7$$
$$c = 18 \times 7$$
$$c = 126$$

The large container weighed 126 ounces.

Remember to check your answer. Replace the variable in the original equation with your solution.

$$c \div 7 = 18$$
$$126 \div 7 = 18$$
$$18 = 18 \checkmark$$

Remember: The two sides will be equal if you have the right answer.

When you have a division problem, make sure you know what question is being asked. Chapter 25 shows how the remainder in division problems can be used in different ways.

Division problems sometimes have a remainder. Read the problem carefully to decide what the problem is asking.

The school band is traveling to an out-of-town concert. There are 102 people who will be traveling as part of the band. Each bus will carry 31 people. Each bus is filled completely before the next bus is loaded.

a. How many buses will be completely filled?

b. How many people will ride on the final bus?

c. How many buses are needed to transport all of the people?

Step 1: Understand the problem.

What do you know?

There are 3 parts to the problem, but the information in the problem is the same.

There are 102 people traveling. A bus can carry 31 people.

What are you trying to find?

Three questions are asked.

How many full buses?
How many people on the last bus?
How many buses are needed?

Division problems can be checked using multiplication.

Step 2: Make a plan.

You can write an equation for this problem.

Step 3: Solve the problem.

The problem involves dividing the people among the buses, so the operation is division.

102 people ÷ 31 people per bus = number of buses

Let b = the number of buses.

$$102 \div 31 = b$$

You know that people and buses must be whole units, so leave the answer in whole numbers, with a remainder.

$$3R9 = b$$

The answer is 3 buses with a remainder of 9 people.

a. How many buses will be completely filled?

3 buses will be completely filled.

b. How many people will ride on the final bus?

When the 3 buses are filled, there will be 9 people remaining to ride in the final bus.

c. How many buses are needed to transport all the people?

You will need to have the 3 full buses, plus one more to carry the remaining 9 people.

$3 + 1 = 4$, so 4 buses are needed.

Step 4: Look back.

Check your computations.
$$31 \times 3 = 93$$
$$93 + 9 = 102 \checkmark$$

Do the answers match the questions? Yes.

Make up a division word problem and explain what the remainder stands for in the answer.

Equations or problems where more than one operation are performed are called multistep. In a multistep problem, you are still trying to get the variable on one side by itself.

Begin with the operation that is farthest from the variable but on the same side of the equal sign. Do the inverse operation on each side of the equation.

Solve for x. $\dfrac{x}{3} - 5 = 2$

Step 1: Write the algebraic equation.

$$\dfrac{x}{3} - 5 = 2$$

Step 2: Look for the operation farthest from the variable but on the same side of the equal sign. You see subtraction (− 5), so do the inverse (addition) first.

$$\dfrac{x}{3} - 5 + 5 = 2 + 5$$

$$\dfrac{x}{3} = 7$$

Step 3: There is only one operation left. It is division, so multiply.

$$\dfrac{x}{3} \times \dfrac{3}{1} = 7 \times 3$$

Step 4: Write the solution.

$$x = 21$$

Step 5: Check the solution. Replace the variable with your solution.

$$\dfrac{x}{3} - 5 = 2$$

$$\dfrac{21}{3} - 5 = 2$$

$$7 - 5 = 2$$

$$2 = 2$$

Remember: To solve for a variable, get the variable alone using the inverse (opposite) operations.

Problem Solving with Multistep Problems

Many problems that use formulas use more than one operation.

John has 20 feet of wire fence to make a rectangular dog pen. He wants the pen to be 4 feet wide and as long as possible. How long can he make the pen?

Step 1: The problem gives you the length of wire fence and the width of the dog pen, and it wants you to find the length. The formula for the perimeter of a rectangle is perimeter = 2(length + width), or $p = 2(l + w)$

Step 2: The formula is your algebraic equation. Replace the variables with the numbers that you are given.
The perimeter (p) = 20 feet and the width = 4 feet

$$p = 2(l + w)$$
$$20 = 2(l + 4)$$

Step 3: Operations outside of parentheses are farther away from the variable than ones that are inside the parentheses. The first number you need to move is multiplied, so divide both sides by that number.

$$\overset{10}{\frac{\cancel{20}}{\cancel{2}}} = \frac{\cancel{2}(l+4)}{\cancel{2}}$$
$$10 = l + 4$$

Step 4: The operation left is addition, so use subtraction.

$$10 - 4 = l + \cancel{4} - \cancel{4}$$

Step 5: Write the solution.
John can make his dog pen 6 feet long.

$$6 = l$$

Step 6: Check the solution.

Take your time; this is not a race!

$$p = 2(l + w)$$
$$20 = 2(6 + 4)$$
$$20 = 2(10)$$
$$20 = 20$$

Writing out an equation in words to model the problem can help you write the correct algebraic equation.

When two numbers are compared, they can be represented as a fraction. Imagine you made 16 out of 20 free throws. You can write the results as a fraction.

$$\frac{\text{number of baskets made}}{\text{number of free throws}} = \frac{16}{20} = \frac{4}{5}$$

This comparison is called a ratio.

Imagine your friend made 8 out of 10 baskets. This comparison can also be written as a ratio.

$$\frac{\text{number of baskets made}}{\text{number of free throws}} = \frac{8}{10} = \frac{4}{5}$$

You and your friend made the same fractional number of baskets. When two ratios are equal, the equation is called a proportion.

$$\frac{16}{20} = \frac{8}{10}$$

Cross Products

The two ratios in a proportion are equal. The cross products of the proportion are also equal. That means if you multiply using a cross, the two products will be equal.

$$\frac{a}{b} = \frac{c}{d} \qquad \frac{a}{b} \diagdown \frac{c}{d} \qquad a \times d = b \times c$$

Look at the example:

$$\frac{16}{20} = \frac{8}{10} \qquad \frac{16}{20} \diagdown \frac{8}{10} \qquad 16 \times 10 = 8 \times 20 \qquad 160 = 160$$

$\frac{a}{b} = \frac{c}{d}$ can be read as "a is to b as c is to d."

A developer who is building a stadium has determined that 3 restrooms will be needed for every 250 seats in the stadium. If there is to be seating for 100,000 people, how many restrooms should be provided?

Step 1: Write the proportion. It may be helpful to set up a table to organize the information before writing the proportion. Let r = total number of restrooms.

restrooms	3	r
seats	250	100,000

$$\frac{3}{250} = \frac{r}{100,000}$$

Step 2: Cross multiply.

$$3 \times 100,000 = 250\,r$$
$$300,000 = 250\,r$$

Step 3: Divide both sides of the equation by 250.

$$\frac{300,000}{250} = \frac{250\,r}{250}$$
$$1,200 = r$$

Step 4: Write the solution.

$$r = 1,200$$

The developer should provide 1,200 restrooms.

Step 5: Check the solution.

Simplify the ratio on the right by dividing the numerator and denominator by 400.

$$\frac{3}{250} = \frac{1,200}{100,000}$$
$$\frac{1,200}{100,000} \div \frac{400}{400} = \frac{3}{250}$$
$$\frac{3}{250} = \frac{3}{250} \checkmark$$

To simplify a ratio is to put the ratio into lowest terms by dividing the numerator and denominator by their common factors.

Percents are ratios that compare a number with 100. The word *percent* means "per hundred." Percents are changed to fractions by removing the percent sign and putting the number over 100. For example:

$$50\% = \frac{50}{100} \qquad 82\% = \frac{82}{100}$$

Percent Problems as Proportions

You can use proportions to solve percent problems. All percent problems are made up of three parts.

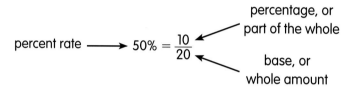

percentage, or
part of the whole

percent rate ⟶ $50\% = \dfrac{10}{20}$

base, or
whole amount

Write the percent rate as a fraction. This will give you a proportion that can be solved using cross multiplication.

50% as fraction ⟶ $\dfrac{50}{100} = \dfrac{10}{20}$

Suppose all jewelry is 25% off. How much is the discount on a $150 necklace?

Step 1: Read the problem.

The discount percent rate is 25%. The whole amount is the regular price of the necklace, $150. The percentage is the amount you are trying to find.

Step 2: Write a proportion.

percent rate ⟶ $\dfrac{25}{100} = \dfrac{x}{\$150}$ ⟵ percentage
(25%) ⟵ whole amount

Percents can be written as fractions or decimals.

Step 3: Cross multiply to solve the proportion for x.

$$\dfrac{25}{100} \diagdown \diagup \dfrac{x}{\$150}$$

$$\$3750 = 100x$$

Step 4: Write the answer.
The discount is $37.50.

$$\$37.50 = x$$

Percent Problems as Equations

You can set up an equation to solve percent problems. You will need to change the percent to a decimal or a fraction.

It is often easier to use decimals than fractions for the percent. Percents are written as decimals by removing the percent sign and moving the decimal point left two spaces.

Students get a 15% discount at the bookstore if they shop on Thursdays. If a book is $24.00, how much will they save on Thursday?

Step 1: Write the equation in words first, then substitute in numbers, variables, and symbols.
15% of $24.00 is how much will be saved.
$15\% \times \$24 = s$

Step 2: Change the percent to a decimal. $15\% = 0.15$

Step 3: Multiply to solve for s. $0.15 \times \$24 = s$

Step 4: Write the answer.
The students will save $3.60. $\$3.60 = s$

Any problem can be solved when you take it one step at a time.

Further Reading

Books

Abramson, Marcie. *Painless Math Word Problems* there is now a 2010 paperback edition. Hauppauge, N.Y.: Barron's Educational Series, 2010.

Watanabe, Ken. *Problem Solving 101: A Simple Book for Smart People.* New York: Penguin Group., 2009.

Zaccaro, Edward. *Becoming a Problem Solving Genius.* Iowa: Hickory Grove Press., 2006.

Zeitz, Paul. *The Art and Craft of Problem Solving.* New Jersey: John Wiley and Sons Inc., 2006.

Internet Addresses

Webmath. <http://www.webmath.com>

Hefferman, Neil. *Ms. Lindquist: The Tutor.* © 2003. <http://www.algebratutor.org>

The Math Forum. *Ask Dr. Math.* © 1994–2003. <http://mathforum.com/dr.math>

Stapel, Elizabeth. *Purplemath—Your Algebra Resource.* ©2000–2003. <http://www.purplemath.com/modules/translat.htm>